MONOLOGUES

Words For Actors

FIFTY PIECES FOR AUDITIONS

Written by Simon O'Corra

FIFTY PIECES FOR AUDITIONS

Here are 50 pieces for audition.

Sharp, punchy, not too long, easy to learn....

Comical, tragic, historical, challenging, confrontational, current....something for everyone.

They have been written (see titles) for men or women, or sometimes either, but it's up to you....challenge the gender!

We hope you find this collection useful and exciting and that you will improve your skills as actors and you may even be able to use one of the pieces for an audition and become a great success!

If you do, we'd love to know about it!

Would you email us and let us know?

socorra@mac.com

TITLES

1. A Deceiver.
2. A Good Deed.
3. A Posh Diamond.
4. A Strong Man.
5. A Useful Act.
6. Activities.
7. AKTION T4
8. An Episode.
9. Baring My Soul.
10. My Story.
11. Big Up.
12. Business As Usual
13. Captain America.
14. Closed For Easter.
15. Decision.
16. Fragile Life.
17. Frightened To Offend.
18. Friends Reunited.
19. Fuckwits.
20. Growing Up.
21. How Do I Fuckin' Eat?
22. I Can Do It.
23. I Am Hopelessly Misunderstood
24. In Hiding.
25. The Key To The Door.
26. Let It Go.
27. Make Me Jean Harlow.
28. Martin.
29. Master Turn.
30. Men.
31. Murder Is A Business.
32. My Cabaret.
33. 9 Lives Od A Munitions Worker
34. Of Course I Am To Blame
35. Painted Lavvy.
36. Rabbit Stew.
37. Regrets.
38. Saving A Life.
39. Speaking Out.
40. Splitting The Difference.
41. The Artist.
42. The Fairer Sex.
43. The Grass Is Greener.
44. The Interview.
45. The Queue.
46. Trapped.
47. The Joys Of A Tiara.
48. The Devil Is On My Shoulder.
49. Who's In Charge?
50. Was Only Tryin' To Help

1. A Deceiver. (f)

I happen to be a good actress.

It helps in luring the unsuspecting into parting with their hard-earned cash.

Now then, don't you be thinking bad of me. I'm fifteen and this is not a sexual thing I am doing. I would never do that, well not yet...............who knows in time!

There are plenty of people out there who are looking for other ways to make themselves feel good and help a poor young acting student.

I started off after I had to give up my acting lessons. Austerity hit home and I was left with little choice but to improve myself. Mum and Dad on zero hour contracts were shafted to be honest and as for me and my needs well.............

I was always told I had great sincerity as an actress so I thought why not use that to get what I need.

So as far as these people know. I'm in a children's home, only just though, as these services are at breaking point. Everyone understands this but rarely do people engage at this time, what I need to do is build the layers of misfortune a wee bit more.

So in a children's home, no parents, or none to speak of, no money of my own, but great talent according to my teachers, who I conveniently no longer see 'cos I lost my place at the college. Cut backs I say...............

If only I could just get some money together to re-join my course, then I'd have some hope.

Mugs the lot of em, 'cos people think I have hope they are willing to support me, unlike those undeserving poor, you see down the job centre. You just need to dangle a prospect of success in from of their noses. Then it reflects well on them.

Needless to say, I have no intention of going to acting lessons anymore. Why would I if I can get rich now?

I'm just a deceiver..........

2. A Good Deed. (m/f)

I opened my door to a woman in a state.

I knew though that something was wrong, apart from the state of this lovely wee puppy she cradled in her arms. Beaten black and blue, scared witless and with what seemed like a broken leg.

This woman did a lot of work for the RSPCA, not rescue work you understand, just fundraising and such. She lived on the outskirts of the village and was a bit of a dark horse. It did seem strange why she would come to me with this poor damaged baby though. Maybe like so many people she thought as I an artist, I must be sensitive.

Or as it transpired, she thought me a soft touch. HA! HA! People can be so bloody stupid.

(pause)

Well she'd come to the wrong person. She had some yarn about having been out for a walk on the coast road and having found the little dog in a hedgerow. She had scooped it up apparently and brought it to me straight away, in a kind of panic.

(pause for thought)

I did wonder why she had been walking on the coast road in pale pink stilettos though and them with not a mark on them.

(looking skeptical)

I nodded concernedly and made all the right noises and most importantly I took the puppy from her and told her to leave everything to me. She was full of appreciation and murmured something as she left about "how could these bastards do this to an innocent creature?"

She little knew of course, that I had lived in the village for most of my life and nothing ever escaped me. I knew already that this woman had a dog that she bred from, and not, according to village gossip, in a very ethical way. I also knew that her bitch had recently produced a litter, for which she would be charging £1500 a puppy. Upon closer inspection of this puppy I could see that he had a deformity in his back legs………………and suddenly the penny dropped.

She it seems was one of those bastards who she disparaged so much!

Now where is that number for the RSPCA?

3. A Posh Diamond. (f)

I'm what you'd call 'in genteel poverty'. From a good family, some ancient inherited wealth and status, which has long gone now. Pretensions? I have none. I know how to treat people well and I know about right and wrong, oh and fairness too. It's just that life can get in the way more often than not.

I suppose Rita misunderstood who I was. She is my cleaner. I could see her and her sideways glances when I had spoken of Waitrose delivering and having to ask her to take the delivery as I had to go out. I suppose I shall never live that down. But what I did not have time to say was that it was my son's birthday and as it is only once a year, I give my custom to them.

The even bigger shock for her came I think when I saw her, how would she say it. "Darn Aldi". She stood, motionless as if in a stupor, and this spell was only broken when I said " Hello Rita, How are you?"

Mrs.......Mrs.......Mrs......... That was all she could say. She looked embarrassed about the lack of things in her basket as she stood at the checkout, all the cheapest stuff imaginable lying at the bottom was making her into a much desired for, invisible person.

I was suddenly saddened. I didn't want this woman to feel this way, why should she? She is doing the best she can for her family by cleaning up my mess once a week and many others', I suspect.

Suddenly I had an idea. I didn't think much about the ramifications of it, because I knew it was coming from a good place. I am not rich, I figured, but I can help out this woman.

"Come and talk to me if you're not busy. That is, come on, walk around with me, we never get to talk when you are around at ours".

She was reluctant but I was not for giving in. I looked her in the eye again and suddenly she said "Erm…. Yes alright!

What a giggle we had. I found out all about her as we walked the aisles, and I sneaked in some extra stuff to my basket but actually for her. She didn't know but I was planning to pay for all her produce. Which I did, not without some argument, but I was having none of it.

As we stood outside and concluded our chat, amidst copious amounts of thanks and you shouldn't haves. The one thing which impressed me was the greatest thing about what I just done was not the produce at all.

Rita loved the fact that I took an interest in her and her life and her family.

Something shifted that day for us both.

4. A Strong Man (m)

Of course, they all think they are - strong that is.

Please!!

Put them in an arena and they'll fight their way out. Well sometimes, if the hype matches reality.

Put them in my boudoir and it's like they are different people. Putty in my hands, willing to do anything, submit totally. I have them.

Of course they don't understand that this is what is happening. They always think they are in control. I'm never am an opponent, just someone to submit to their charms.

Fools!!

What is it that overrides this testosterone fueled imperative to kill, to survive, to attack everyone?

Sex! Testosterone fueled of course but even more primal.

This is what I play on in my work. I get what I want by offering what these strong men think they want, more than anything.

I watch them as they proceed, you can almost see them devising the narrative to tell their mates tomorrow.

"I took her, she was gagging for it" he'll say.

I don't need to tell anyone because I know the truth. Of course, I'm telling you but you don't know this man's name or just why he is so important to me. Oh not in any needy way, you understand, just as a means to an end.

A hit.

This last one felt my blade enter him as he entered me. He had some way to go before his job would have been done anyway and I just don't have the time for that nonsense. He gave in too easily and the price was paid.

Job Done.

5. A Useful Act. (f)

I came here to escape the Nazis. I had just completed my medical studies. I was glad to go as I saw my country capitulate and this bothered me greatly.

(incredulous)

You see I had a secret, aside from a hatred of Germans.

Amsterdam became my home, a place untainted by Nazi ideology. For two years I had a happy life, practising medicine and living with my darling girlfriend. Then all changed once again, the spectre, it seemed, had followed me. This time though, the German's wanted *me*, no, not for deportation, but to be in their God-forsaken army.

(unbelieving)

I, a Catholic, was being asked to do their dirty work for them. What was I to do? I did not have long to wait to find out as the Germans found out that I am part Jewish. So they thankfully let me go. I melted back into Dutch society once more.

I became convinced that I must join the Resistance, which I did. I got involved with a group of artists and even worked for an underground newspaper called 'Rat Poison' and we drafted an artist's charter denouncing Nazi censorship.

(looking proud and defiant)

Over the time that we were writing and producing journals, it became imperative to organise some kind of direct action. A small group of us decided to attempt to bomb the Population Registry. This we did and had some small success, all scattering into hiding afterwards. My impulses though were my downfall, so here I am awaiting trial and almost certain death. You see I had to get a message to my darling, I knew how worried she would be, but the Gestapo were watching her and all was lost.

(hanging his head down) and then beginning to write a letter)

Lovely mother, lovely father, I will be killed tomorrow, I...............

(a pause as he realises the protein of this statement)

really had to act like this. I had no other choice. God gives me the power to put up with this situation. I have prepared myself for death.

(a small sob)

Above all I refuse to feel hate or revenge. I will be tough with the help of God and will die as a man if he wants.

(pause)

I believe with this one action I brought more blessing to humanity that I would have done in an entire life as a physician.

(he looks upwards with tears in his eyes and defiance in his soul)

6. Activities. (m/f)

I've got my regular activities session later today.

(*checking her phone*)

What? You have to be bloody kidding me.

You'll never guess what. The bastards.

The sports ground is shut. So finally, they've taken the advice. Loopy bloody lockdown has to start on the day I am supposed to be seeing my girls. We've been meeting all the previous weeks. I just don't get it. Are we in or out? Why can't people tell what's going on for sure. Is that too much to ask?

Worse thing is I've got to spend time ringing around people to tell 'em its off. As if I ain't got better things to do.

Oh fuck, wait a minute, what about Lucy and Alli? They don't have phones. So, what am I supposed to do about them? Do you think I can risk going out now without being stopped by the coppers? The girls live way out too so unless I can get them a message, they'll be liable to be stopped for being out on the streets. They'll freak I can tell ya.

My girls don't need this kind of trouble. Bloody government thinks everyone is well into the 21st century but……………….

not everyone is, there's plenty of folks who ain't got computers and phones.

This is just a right old pisser.

Well BoJo, I'm just gonna have to do your job for you. I'll sort your mess out.........

You know I bet there must be hundreds of people like me picking up the pieces of this mess. It's good job though eh........

7. AKTION T4. (m)

My paranoia left me as soon as I lost my job here and became a patient instead. All my cares left as I settled a domesticity. The only trouble I encountered now were vicious jibes from the orderly, a brute of a man, who had witnessed my apparent downfall. This pleased him as the balance of power had shifted. I simply did not care anymore, but he still thought I did for some reason.

(smiling)

Albrecht is my lover,

(embracing himself as though he were embracing Albrecht)

he is the reason I am in here.

(a silent pause)

Once I got the role of superintendent at the hospital, strange things started to happen. My assistant began walking past my house on his way to the hospital, something he had never done before. This confused me. He also began to challenge my practice at times, concerning my mania patients.

(looking confused)

This seemed to be because I had struck up a particular intense working relationship with Albrecht, a patient, whose only problem seemed to me, after consulting with Magnus Hirschfeld, at the Institute of Sexology, was one of being at variance with the prevailing heterosexual norm, for instance a homosexual. He was actually only suffering from society and its dictates.

(looking unsurprised)

Our friendship deepened and I was spending more and more time with him discussing philosophy, mathematics, history and the Classics. This of course took me away from other patients to an extent, but my interactions with Albrecht seemed to affect such changes in him I was proud of the success I was having.

During this time, I found myself loving him, indeed more so than I had ever loved my work. He had become my life's passion. We were often heard to discuss the works of Plato and others, and this, unbeknownst to me, was brought up by my assistant, again and again, with the Board of Governors.

Eventually they demanded a meeting to request that I cease working with the mania patients, especially Albrecht. I refused of course and thought that would be the end of it, but my covetous assistant, a member of the new National Socialist Party, now had the ammunition he needed to raise questions about my own mental state. The very next day when I arrived at the hospital, I was accosted by two orderlies and forcibly led to the mania ward, where once stripped, I was shackled to my new bed and left to bemoan my situation. Albrecht comforted me but I was remarkably calm.

(at peace)

In a sense I had what I wanted now.

(coming to his senses)

I have recently overheard talk of a new *treatment* centre called T4 in Brandenburg. We can all expect to be taken there it seems. Albrecht was taken there yesterday in what they called a *Charitable Bus,* with large windows. I watched him leave and waved him goodbye until tomorrow.

(looking melancholy)

I am due to be taken there tomorrow for *treatment* too.

8. An Episode. (m)

(shouting)

Go on just go away, go play with Jimmy. I just need a break for five minutes. Please………..

(lifting a coffee cup to his lips, looking totally worn out)

I've been feeling a bit breathless today. Stress I suppose. I had it a lot back in 2008. I recognise the feeling.

(looking worried and feeling his chest, near his heart)

I've four kids in lockdown. It's too much really and it's only been two weeks so far.

(panting, eyes widening and acting very restless)

It's all up to me. The wife's a nurse. I'm on my own. We don't see her. She has to do her duty I suppose. But I've been so used to her coming home after a shift to help with the house husband thing. You see I've never quite got used to it, 12 years and still counting. I was a banker before.

(breathing heavily to try to compensate and the starting to cry)

Oooh! Oooh! OOOH!

(shivering and sobbing)

Oh My God what am I gonna do?

(grabbing his chest and beginning to breathe more deeply).

Come on breathe,, you fool, breathe. Think of the kids. You have to stay strong. Everyone is saying that. It assumes that everyone is strong of course, which makes many of us feel even weaker. I came close to suicide back in the Crash and you never quite lose that feeling.

(panting and then deepening his breathing and slowly calming down)

That's a bit better. Phew! God knows where I'd be without these breaks sitting on my kid's   trampoline.

What a way to go eh!

(suddenly laughing and laughing)

It beats crying that's for sure.

A heart attack in the midst of a Virus Pandemic Lockdown. What a choice!

Come on get a grip!

Jimmy, kids come on.

9. Baring My Soul. (m)

Fuck! What am I doing here?

(wringing his hands)

Why did I ever agree to this?

(looking side to side nervously)

"What could go wrong?" That's what the counsellor said. He was laughing.

It's alright for him. Bloody gym bunny, perfect skin and the coiffured hair.

"Go on try it" he said. "It's a jump off the deep end but they are there to draw you, that's all."

In theory I agree with him. But. From my side it's a massive step.

He hasn't got a leg missing and a mass of burns over his body. He hasn't lost his wife who can't bear to look at him anymore.

(angry)

Fuck! Fight for your country they say. We'll look after you they said. That's as maybe. but what about the effect of *this*....

(looking down at his body)

on my wife. Not to mention those folks out there. Waiting for a great model to help them become better artists, and just getting me. I can spot the vomiters a mile off. There'll be plenty of stiff upper lip I can tell you. They should suffer for their art after all.

And. What do I get out of this. "Self-esteem" he says. "A sense of achievement" he insists.

Well what it feels like to me is a bloody nightmare.

(pause and the beginnings of a stiff upper lip)

So here goes. Ready or not.

10. My Story. (m)

I cannot see!……..My God I cannot see! *(gulping)*

I can smell and taste the gas; it is burning my insides. *(Grabbing at his chest)* NO! I have to keep calm, what was it the sergeant told us? "Keep calm and think of a good time in your life, think of your sweethearts or your wives or your kids."

I can feel the mud and the water all around me now. I can hear it too. Oh God what is happening to me. "No, no think of something nice, stay calm". The sergeant said so.

I remember a Summer not so long ago when I was back home…….oh no…… "don't talk about home, you can think of it but don't say it out loud." *(pause)* But I have to talk about it, it's too mad to just think of it especially when I cannot see. It's too final and too vast to remain quiet when the lights have gone out. *(breathing calmly)*

That's it. I was with Tommy, yes that was his name, funny really, but he was my Tommy not just any old *Tommy.* There was mud back then too, down by the pond, we were alone and we'd been skinny dipping. It was our first time in more ways than one. The mud was cool and the water lapped around our legs. No one else was around. No one knew where we were. There was a burning inside then too, the first time I had ever felt this way. It was intense not like this shitty mustard gas, which I know is ripping my insides out, but an outside in kind created by another's presence.

ARGH!!!!!!!! *(breathing deeply and in great pain)*

I've seen those great blisters on men's backs. Hideous giant yellowish pustules.

I am done for but I have to tell my story, just once. *(deep breathing)*

Mine and Tommy's skins were brand new, untouched, virginal and ripe. Suddenly men not boys. We had explored each other then, with a certainty which, had Tommy survived the Somme, we would have spent the rest of our lives doing, sure in our love. Something blossomed that day and it was a magical feeling, snuffed out all too fast.

Oh the pain is getting worse, the pain of the gas, the rot in my feet, the nibbling rats who know I'm a goner. *(writhing in agony)* All this pestilence has me in its grip. *(resigned now)*

Who will know my story now? No one can know my history? Tommy is dead and pretty soon I will be too. Our love will die to the world. Not even forgotten just unknown.

11. Big Up. (f)

Misunderstood! Me? No way!

What you see is what you get.

(brushing her collar with her fingers, acting proud)

No pussyfooting around here.

I know how life works and business too, as you can see. I learnt the hard way.

My staff will tell ya, "oh yeah she's strict, but we know where we are. Look at the business she has built up from nothing." They beam with pride when they say "Madam's a Marvel!"

They know they couldn't have done it themselves. It takes a certain type of person you see.

It's true. I did it all myself. Well not completely of course, no one ever builds a corporation like mine without a dedicated workforce and a good accountant. These people keep you grounded after all and they respect you all the more, when they can feel respected themselves.

Don't cross me though, never do that. I haven't built all this up to have some wide boy think they can take what's mine. If you think you can then go ahead, but I can see a rat coming a mile off, and in fact their smell usually precedes them.

Anyone thinks they can get away with calling me babe, sugar, darling, you just walk on by too.

It's Madam to you, one and all. There is no other greeting I respond to, given I have no husband nor kids, who might get away with something different. This is my business and I don't free talk with anyone in it.

12. Business As Usual. (m)

I'm not sure what to do! Who would be?

I'm the one who usually has the strategy in place, the action plan prepared and the resources stored away as a kind of contingency. This means it can always be business as usual at Sun Dew Care Homes. But now.

As I said I don't know what to do. I am living and working here now.

I miss my kids so much and being able to share the load with my wife.

My poor family have not seen me for weeks, since long before the supposed lockdown. I feel so isolated and under pressure.

I have never seen the like before.

Each day is spent in caring within a small team for 16+ hours usually.

This whole affair has me caught out for the first time in my Management career. I'm quite hands on at the best of times but have never done this to such an extent, caring face to face. I mean, if you can call it that. I have to ask each resident to move back as far as they can into their rooms in order to leave their food on a makeshift table. It so in-human to me.

You know, at the beginning even before this virus was news, within the first week I had 17 out of a 25 strong staff team off sick. Common sense told me to tell them not to come in.

"STAY HOME" I said and way before the Government had even adopted this as their mantra. I have always run a tight ship regards illness. We care for vulnerable people, the last thing we want is an outbreak, like the one we are going through now.

Its like being on a desert island, like from a shipwreck, and I am slowly seeing other survivors, all isolated in their own islets, succumb to the worst this damn disease can throw at them.

The only bonus if bonus it can be called is that my work load is lessening each day. We are down to 21 now from 38. It's a scandal really but we are doing our best. We open the doors to funeral directors at the end of each shift and they remove bodies, 2 or 3 a day. I am not sure how much longer we will even need to do that.

I have to take more and more risks now as PPE is unavailable it seems and all bank staff are now transferred to the NHS.

I sometimes wonder if I shall be in one of those bags one of those days........

13. Captain America. (m/f)

(looking around the room and suddenly seeing Captain America, and picking him up and looking at him lovingly)

I have fond memories of him. That's not something that comes easy to me, memories I mean, well not since the accident. It's all a bit of a jumble, well, a *lot* of one really, friends help me out all the time and me Mam too. Funny how I miss my Nana, and can see her clear as day anytime.

Dylan's my star. Dylan the Villain – he keeps me going, with his licks and antics. What a prize pooch he is!

(Examining Captain America)

This takes me back to a simpler time. We had to be frugal back then and ever so slightly tricksy to make some magic for the kids.

(making Captain America fly)

Here I am in lockdown and you know, it's like being back there, in the 1970s I mean. Till recently I found the world totally overwhelming but this isolation makes me smile in so many ways. I am managing far better, life is simpler being isolated, although I don't wish anyone any harm because of it. But isn't it strange that it takes something like this to bring us back to our senses?

(looking fondly at Captain America)

Wildlife is coming back and did you see the clear waters in Venice a couple of weeks ago? There is no more smog in China either and that freeway in Los Angeles, you know the one, in that film, where Michael Douglas totally lost it, that's blooming empty these days. There is no more road rage there. I like all that very much, and you know I think the world is liking it too.

14. Closed For Easter. (m)

So the Olympics is cancelled! Wimbledon too! But Easter? Really?

What am I supposed to do? I normally race away to the coast on Easter Monday 'cos let's face it, being a vicar at Easter is tough going. We've normally had weeks of Lent and then a full-on weekend devoted to our Lord Jesus, oh - and the congregation. So now I'll be staying in and contemplating my own navel and then, staying home some more 'cos the south coast may as well be in Timbuktu, for all the means I have to get there.

(pausing to remember something he just said)

Well, in talking about my congregation, here in South London, numbers are falling. I'm never sure quite why, but they are. The church it seems is useful for its charity work but people are worn down with austerity and it's hard to hang around for our Lord to make things right. Or at least for some. Lord knows what will happen now that Easter is cancelled - a whole year with our Lord not being Risen again. How do I explain this to my flock? These things have been a given for centuries, even millennia. How now can they be cancelled? This is unprecedented and raises all sorts of questions about religion in the same way as this virus is making us think about what it important in our lives.

What can I do though? How do I reach my flock?

(head in hands)

Wait! I have an old video camera somewhere, I could at least say Mass; my sermons are ready after all.

(pausing to think)

But what do I do with the film when I have made it? A lot of my folks don't have computers and I've never got around to making the parish a Facebook page. No one can go out of their houses, and who has a video player anymore? It's at times like these that you wish you had gotten more organised and learnt how to operate the technology.

(pausing to think)

When I face a quandary I often ask "What would Jesus do"

I think that he would say do it anyway, even if the people cannot see the Mass, hear the sermon, do it for yourself and to honour God. I can at least get word out that I am doing it, so they feel connected. That is what life is about after all.

Connectedness in an unconnected world.

15. Decision. (f)

I'm a Leitrim girl. It's in my blood, good farming stock is my heritage. The land calls to me.

(looking back fondly)

Oldham Below Town was never part of that picture in my mind.

(looking scared)

We managed to survive through the famine, God knows how. I suppose we had some of our own land which was enough. Some of the family though had settled in Lincolnshire during the famine period and they spoke of a more certain and settled life than most had in Ireland.

I was tempted I have to say and ended up in the countryside once again, only this time in England.

(looking resignedly happy)

I missed my birthplace and my Da and Ma, but I made it work for me. Some years in I met a man, from Mayo he was, who omitted to tell me he really lived in Oldham. and was only visiting his people in Brigg. He was a good 'un or so I thought. He definitely had the talk. I married him and before I knew it, I was living in working in a cotton mill. And yes, you guessed it, it was in Oldham.

(looking surprised)

How had this happened?

(Looking non-plussed)

Four daughters and the two of us, living in a back to back, in a grimy town, where life was all about working and sleeping. The air was heavy with soot and smog. I missed the sky, the rolling countryside yes even tending the livestock.

(experiencing a pleasant memory)

It took my daughter, my namesake, Bridget, to steal us away back to the Lincolnshire countryside, when she married a visiting chap she met in an Oldham Park. The decision was made for me on that day.

Those Oldham days were bad, but in a way, they make me grateful for the time I now spend in my home from home.

16. Fragile Life. (f)

What a witch!

Mr Storr, my great grandfather, took her as his second wife, and he, only widowed not two weeks. It was soon known that she beat the children daily and scolded her amiable husband often. When he was widowed, he had to find a new wife to look after his needs and make sure his brood behaved themselves. He and the children got even more than they bargained for with the witch, as she took the farm right from under everyone's noses.

That must be why Martha got away from home so quickly I suppose. Sometime later her younger sister ran away to America too, driven by fear and loathing no doubt, but no one has heard anything of her since. She must have been desperate to go all that way on her own.

Martha had found her Saviour, Richard, a carman and hawker, passing through her village. He spoke of having good prospects and he was a jovial fellow. They married.

She ended up running an inn with him. However, the temptation of the liquor for the rogue was just too much. Martha's eyes were soon opened I can tell you. What a life she must have had……….

As for now, Aunt Martha lays so wide from us. The last news we had was that he had brought them all down to poverty.

Aunt Hannah had been to see the old man on his deathbed and she said he was laid low in a very wicked state, and had been for a long time. She told us all that her mother had a weighty handful of him at the end, and he left her with nothing to rely on except some parish relief. Apparently, the old girl was embittered and distant.

No wonder I suppose…………..

After his death I wrote to her wishing her to come amongst us for a few months. We would have paid all her expenses and given her some clothes. We could have been a comfort to her.

I thought her very unkind and proud as she never answered me.

So whether she be still living in Castleford or she has gone amongst her children we just don't know. I can only hope that she did not end up in the workhouse……………..

How fragile life is!

17. Frightened To Offend. (m/f)

This older man wants to show me a piece of his work!

(holding a printed script up)

He's a writer and a baby boomer! That's what he says anyway.

What is that exactly? People keep banging on about it, it's a bloody silly phrase though. He's about as far from being a baby as one could get.

Anyway, I thought it would be good to see his work. It's good for us young 'uns to show our support isn't it.

I saw on his website that he wrote a lot about the war and the Holocaust urgh!,

(looking skeptical)

but I still thought I'd give it a go. He might have put a positive spin on it. If not, it's not like I would be obliged to add it to the anthology. Anyway, I can always make up some cool shit about being worried about offending people to avoid using the work.

So, he sent it over this morning and I printed it off, which proved a waste of paper, 'cos just as I thought - Fuck what am I supposed to with this? It's bloody depressing for starters, I just want to think about positive things and our anthology is not setting out to upset people after all. There is too much bollocks going on in the world right now; my phone has died for starters, without giving room to some shitty historical stuff that has no relevance to what is happening today.

We need to forget all that horror, we can't do anything about it, and there lots of people who doubt it all happened like they say it did. We don't want to upset anyone do we? We need just to focus on getting through the next few weeks and months, until we can get back to normal. It's time for us, the young people, to see if we can do a better job than his generation did.

After all he had his chance when he was my age to change the world.

Time to let it all go, old man.

(dropping script in the bin)

18. Friends Reunited. (m)

Drawn to what hurts us!

(laughter)

I read that somewhere. Like drawn to sugar when we know it messes with our bodies, like getting pissed or smoking way too much.

(pointing to himself)

Well it's a few years ago now when *Friends Reunited* popped up and I thought, well given that I had a shit time at school, why not look up some of those school bullies. I wish I could say it was either a mistake or a great thing. To an outsider it would seem like utter madness, but after years having elapsed, I needed to know that this dull pain I had still, was linked to some people and not just in my imagination.

I put myself on there and started to look round for the years I was at school to see who was on. I found an old girlfriend, now married and a receptionist at a dentist's; I found an old bum chum too, although he soon told me to sling my hook. He too was married now and did not want his gay past brought up again, Like I would cause any trouble to anyone. It there is one thing being bullied taught me, that it's not worth seeking revenge. Or was it 4 years of counselling that gave me that revelation?

Fuck! My life was hell back then.

(emotional)

I lived in a state of permanent fear and anger all mixed up together. I never knew where the next slap, thump or stream of verbal abuse would come from.

(looking over his shoulder nervously)

This was a place I had to go to. If I had played truant then the home punishment would have been dreadful. It was the perfect trap and there was no one to tell about it. My Dad's response was fight back, not good when you are not a fighter by personality.

Anyway, back to Friends Reunited, I did say hello to a few of the perpetrators but they were all sweetness and light, like nothing happened right. Only John apologised for terrorising me, which was kind of ok, but we still didn't have anything in common.

In all it was disappointing exercise but I did take comfort in just how boring most people's lives had become, weighed down by families, keeping them in a place. I have taken control of my life and I am happy. It took years though and those are times I cannot get back, though heaven knows I try.

19. Fuckwits. (m/f)

The fuckwits. Those fucking Independent advocates. Yeah, they are nice enough people, don't get me wrong. But where do they get their ideas from. You don't think they are actually socialists, do you? Oh fuck!

Of course, we do have policies and procedures for abuse but we don't really want someone using them, now do we? They're not there for our patients, oops sorry I mean clients. They are all part of our marketing strategy. It makes people feel secure that's all. The Advocacy Service is part of an advertising campaign too, it reassures people that we want to know their concerns. This is a business after all. Bums on seats and all that.

Our advocate is called Beverley, can you believe it a bloke called Beverley. Of course, we are not going to do anything about any suggestions he may make. We have to keep the upper hand after all. I suppose he will insist we sort out various things for the patien,,,,,,….. sorry clients. Well he can fuck off. At the end of the day if things don't fit our plans then its tough titties.

Let's face it. Old people are a fucking nuisance anyway. Nice to have a cup of tea with, well for about a couple of minutes. They're all dementing these days. They've been out of real life for so long they have nothing to contribute.

So here we are……..

(holding up a letter)

A fucking independent advocate making a formal complaint about some abuse they've witnessed. To be honest I've witnessed worse myself, yet I don't complain do I. These tossers don't know what it takes to run a care home.

Mrs. Arnold had it coming anyway, she is a vicious cow at times. No need to bring in her daughter about this though. She doesn't care much anyway.

So, bin it is……………well not actually of course, but we'll have Bev the wanker on some technicality and hopefully he'll just fuck off. The police and social services can be invaluable in this. Then it'll be business as usual.

20. Growing Up. (f)

Anonymity is what I said I had sought. Me! Now a famous writer.

Strange you might think for a dancer and an actress to seek such a thing. If I am honest those creative avenues I tried before had not really worked out for me, and I needed time to think about my future and a place to explore my creativity.

(Smiling cheekily)

Buenos Aires was the place to be and maybe I actually wanted excitement and opportunity although I could not say that, not in this society.

(Defiant)

The city was a great place for me to live. I found a lover, a political man at the centre of things and all seemed set fair for me with him, until I found out he was married. Adultery for men it seemed was alright, even allowed, but not for it to go anywhere otherwise.

(looking disappointed)

This episode in my life affected me greatly and informed my politics especially when it concerned my gender, which was revealed again later when I found myself pregnant by a journalist colleague who of course did not want the child we had created together. I knew that I wished to keep the child and I did.

(looking proud)

These Little little men, which I have written about, gave me confidence as a woman; men could hurt and men could betray and I knew this first hand and our society allows them to do it. I knew though that it was possible for a woman to make her own way. This is what I have done in my life always.

(looking pleased with herself)

I persevered and from this effort and passion I have achieved a kind of greatness for myself and in myself. Published works have multiplied for me: poetry, articles, journal excerpts and many other things, with many prizes being forthcoming.

My voice was still a little stilted until I found drama once more, not as an actor this time but as a writer. This gave me the ability to talk of the subjects I had written about. To take my words into an active zone, to make them vocal, to make them human and to make them *REAL.*

21. How Do I Fuckin' Eat? (m)

"What ya mean you have no fuckin' food? You're a fuckin food bank. I always get me food here. I'm entitled."

I was in her fuckin' face and I had no fuckin' mask on either. HA! She hated that, actually pulled away from me like I'm a fucking' leper. She don't like me and I don't like her especially after I heard her saying out the back " He could do to do without some food for a few weeks, have you seen the size of him. "Fuckin' cheek.

She had no room to talk she wasn't exactly a fuckin' super model 'erself.

"We've been robbed and the little bleeders have taken everything." she moaned and she was giving me the evils. Fuck knows why?

"When can I get some fuckin' scran then?" I shouted out. She pulled away from me again. Fuck! She's jumpy.

EWW!

She got *La di da* all of a sudden.

"We don't know when to expect another delivery. All the supermarkets are struggling because those greedy idiots are raiding their shelves"

"How do I fuckin' eat then?" I said "How do I fuckin' get through the next week?" She looked me up and down and only just stopped 'erself from commenting, I could see.

"Why haven't you got a mask on? Think of COVID 19" she said

"COVID 19, You avin' a laugh, I can't deprive the world of this face" I said "I might miss out on a shag."

She raised her eyebrows as if to say "Right, whatever!"

"You need one of them full body suits, love" says I "'cos lets face it your shaggin' days are over."

"Right" She screams "Out"

"Oh, and by the way if you want to eat, go and see your mates, they stole the stuff, Tell em they're on CCTV. Byeeee, Have a nice life".

"Fuckin' Cheek" I says" I suppose my Food Bank days are numbered."

She nodded.

The bitch.

22. I Can Do It. (f)

He keeps saying "You'll never do it. You have no training, no formal education. Who are you kidding."

(nervous laugh)

I keep telling him that my teacher is very pleased with me and I will be amazing in the play.

"You showing off in front of people. BAH?" he snipes back at me.

It's not showing, off its acting.

(flustered and giggling)

I have been working towards this for months. I know its only amateur dramatics

(light giggle born of excitement)

but it's a start and I want to give it all I have.

"Well I hope you don't let things slip here. I worry about that. "he moans

He worries about that? When was the last time he lifted a finger?

Oh yeah, I remember now he made me a cup of tea the day our Robert was born.

I don't try to stop him doing owt. He plays a mean guitar and yet does he ever do anything with that skill.? No! I always say to him, go on give it a go. There was a group a while ago who were looking for a guitar player but he said no.

(Laughter)

I am going ahead though 'cos anyway he hasn't enough energy to stop me and our Robert is all for it. I just wish he had some positive things to say about me doing this, getting on with my long-cherished dream.

Tim, who's my co-star, is great with me, so giving, as I think they say in the business. He shares the play with me truly.

(pause and then laughter and then sadness)

I wish my man shared in the same way……………..

23. I'm Hopelessly Misunderstood. (f)

Look let me speak. Please! Thank you.

I have to clear this up. I can't have people thinking I'm homophobic.

There is no need for eye rolling. I am mortified that you or anyone else thinks I might be anti-gay.

AH! Please.

(raises her hand)

No give me a chance to explain. Come on I deserve that at least. You bloody minorities are always getting your say.

Your eyes will stay like that if a wind gets up. What have I said now? It's true anyway.

You don't hear me banging on about who I go to bed with.

Look stop that.

When have you ever heard me talking about the sex Dennis and I have? You must admit your lot do like to talk sex, along with your interior design, those ridiculous little dogs and bloody musicals.

Don't get me wrong you're all very entertaining at times. But listen: the operative words here are *At Times*. It just gets a bit much. I'm not sure that clients always like it. It's nothing I wouldn't to say to Lucy, if she were going on about her bloke all the time. We're a team after all and I do like to treat everyone the same.

What are you doing? Now come on don't be silly. Oh, come on don't be like that. I just wanted to clear the air.

Where are you going?

Well I didn't see that coming. He's our best hairdresser too, by far.

Lucy? What………..Where are you going?

What did I say?

(head in her hands)

I'm so hopelessly misunderstood.

24. In Hiding. (m)

I never imagined this would happen to *me*. No nor *my* family.

Why do humans often end up in hiding? Why can't we all roam free?

Thank heaven for some good people, who have agreed to hide us here. You'd never guess where we are?

Right above us during the day, there are men working on trucks for the company. No one knows we are here except the foremen. We sleep during the night, as my husband's a snorer or we read. But we must remain alert during the day. We cannot afford to make a sound. It's hard I can tell ya 'cos the little 'uns get restless.

This hole has been here since the 1930s, that's how long people around here have needed sanctuary for. The foreman's Papa was a good man. He built this place for those times when some humans needed to hide, for whatever reason. Not those who had actually done wrong of course, but those wrongly accused for all manner of reasons.

You know I look back at that Diary by that girl, what was her name, Anne Frank, I think. We read that in school. She hid in a small space with 8 or 9 others for more than two years! How was that possible? We've only been here for two or maybe three days, I lose track. As I said it's tough and there's no sign of when it will end, or how we can get free again, at least round here.

How could another human being force someone into hiding like that, what gives them the right. Same right I suppose as the one where they assume they can accuse who they like.

Us Americans, all of us, fought a war so that that kind of thing would never happen again and yet here I am hiding away from an injustice.

It eats at your soul this confinement, it wears you down, it must I suppose break you, like it did Anne Frank and countless others.

None of those people did anything wrong, yet this prison is the only choice they have.

25. The Key To The Door. (m/f)

Well here it is at last. I am 21. It's my 21st. So?

(looking bemused)

I get it! But why is it so important to some people.

(searching for an answer)

My Mum the fount of all knowledge. Just says it's my 21st, a big birthday.

(looking quizzically)

But why is it BIG?

My Gran is different, she says I'll get the key to the door.

(bemused and unknowing)

What Key? What door?

(Shaking and then scratching his head)

I asked her and she said…. You Know……..Erm, no I don't know.

I can see a range of keys on all my birthday cards. But what the fuck…….

(staring intently)

does it mean?

Gran did say it's when all things used to change. Argh! Now I get it. She is talking about the past. But does it still mean the same now?

(throwing hands in the air)

I am living at home with Mum and Dad still. No chance of that changing anytime soon. So, it can't mean a key to a new flat or even a house. I've already got a car so I don't need a key for that. The car came when I was 18 - another big birthday that people go on about. I have no idea what else I might need a key to. Maybe being 21 is a different thing these days, who knows. I certainly don't!

26. Let It Go. (m)

Gay marriage is legal here. Thank goodness! It even is in America. We all just get on with our lives now. So...............

(raising arms in despair)

Why at this time during this pandemic are volunteer staff working at Central Park's Emergency Hospital in NYC, being asked to recite an oath that involves a denial of gay marriage. Priorities guys!!!!

What kind of warped mentality in the midst of this global health crisis, insists on focusing people's energy on such a thing?

(incredulous)

I'm a male nurse, and believe me, anything other than the status of my patients' health and my ability to carry on caring, is not even registering in my mind. If I was asked right now before I went on shift to declare an oath against who a person is, my response would include the words FUCK and OFF.

My husband is in isolation from me, although not from everyone else, he is doing his job. He is a consultant, and staying at a newly rented house close to the hospital. I get to go to our home in between shifts and I miss him terribly especially at this time of anguish and uncertainty, but at least our life together is recognised, not under threat and not part of some agenda which is not even dropped when thousands are dying globally.

Priorities are important but recognising what is a valid one at any given time is crucial if we are all to survive these times.

Humanity needs humanity now more than ever.

27. Make Me Jean Harlow. (f)

Platinum Blonde is not quite my thing. It would wash me out I think, and Mother would never allow it anyway. I could have her wavy hair though!

(stroking her hair looking in a mirror)

Jean Harlow's look is what I loved. Such a shame she died in '37. I was devastated. It's the look I am choosing for tonight though.

(pushing at her cheeks and lips in the mirror)

This afternoon we were being taught how to change our look. So interesting and exciting.

"You need to look sophisticated not trampy," snapped my sister. As though she had any idea about what an actress' look meant. Truus is older than me but I know more than her.

(looking proud)

She is going for a Paulette Goddard image. But. She is such a goody-two-shoes, compared to Jean. I suppose my sister will feel more comfortable and that is important though.

I'm 17 and my sister is 19. It's 1942. We need to be presentable of course. We have outgrown our ringlets and pretty little dresses. We have stopped handing out leaflets, as that is too dangerous now, we can no longer expect to get by just by being a cutie pie anymore. We need elegance and poise now.

(posing)

Tonight, we are trying something different. Something we have never done before.

(taking the audience into her confidence)

We are going to a bar. I suppose you may be smiling at this, as it's what so many girls our age start to do. But we have a special reason..........

(pause)

We shall meet some boys at the bar, invite them for a romantic walk and when we are strolling along...........

Then I shall kill him. A Nazi boy..............

28. Martin. (f)

Who the hell does she think she is?

(shaking her fist)

I'm as good as the next girl. I'm a look, quite the catch.

(hands on hips)

My Martin's got a mind of his own. He's lovely. I adore him. We have a good laugh together. That's if she'd ever stop trying to keep us apart. He's mine. So what if he's my first cousin. Them royals' get away with it all the time.

(her nose in the air)

She'd better watch out, mother or no, I'll get her back.

I'm not afraid of her, I'll give her what for. I can fight like the best of 'em.

(throwing a punch and almost falling over)

I'm gonna raise a bit of a fuss at the next get together. Everyone knows what she's doing with her youngest. The things bloody widows get up to, she won't be so sure of herself then, when It's out in the open.

They share a bed you know, her and her John, he's never married, 'cos he's getting it at home. HA!

Martin needs to get away from that pair of sinners. I need to convince him. She's got him under her spell. He should come with me. I love him. I'm the best thing for him. Lizzie, in the village has set her cap at him, but she's a slut. Been with everybody that one. He'll realise once I tell everyone.

I'm gonna make sure I get my Martin and she'll get her comeuppance, that Ma of his.

It makes my blood boil it does. People always interfering, it's a bloody nuisance.

29. Master Turn. (m)

Ladies, Gentlemen and Children! Welcome to...... ....

(looking stunned, serious, bemused, sad, start of an internal dialogue, an absence)

Look at the lady of the trapeze - nah don't bother - check out her husband. He's the real deal.

(empassioned)

Those tights leave nothing to the imagination. Meat and two veg and some.

(upset)

He can't be wearing a jock strap. I've told him about that before. He thinks it keeps the punters coming,

(happy again)

well it would me, if I were a punter,

(angry again)

but it leaves nothing at all to the imagination. You have to have a bit of mystery, I think. His missus is not too keen either. She regards it has hers I suppose, stupid cow.

(Jolly)

If you've got it flaunt it. So long as he can catch her, I don't care. I get to ogle him from the safety of the ground.

(a thoughtful pause)

The clowns do my head in too. You know what they say, big feet means big…………… that's only true in the case of one of em. They mess about in and out of costume and I often sneak a peak in their changing rooms. I'm in the know as they say. Wonder if you can guess who's got the biggest schlong? No?

(looking surprised)

It's Adolphe of course. He knows what to do with it as well. There's a reason why Hector, you know the little one, walks like that. If you use your imagination please.

(looking imperious)

They were at it the other day bold as brass. Butter wouldn't melt with Adolphe's Whiteface Pierrot. It's the serious ones you have to watch out for. He is so snobby and sure of himself. Well if the audience has seen him last Wednesday afternoon his cover would have been blown that's for sure.

(suddenly back to life and facing a crowd of disbelieving punters)

…………..the Circus one and all…………..

30. Men. (f)

Bloody hell!

Here we go again. Meeting yesterday was cancelled because the chair has man flu. He's the only bloody man on the committee and once again for this month nothing can happen.

We're quorate too for goodness sake, but no he puts his foot down, throws his toys out of his pram and we all, each one of us fuming, have to get back on the various trains we have travelled across the country in and return to our families, and by implication, our domestic duties. That's what the old bastard means when he says these things.

It never ceases to amaze me just how much men will let organisations slide towards ruin even, rather than give up their right to control what happens, especially to women. I swear this one is trying to stop us from voting on what needs to happen now that the museum is struggling. This is a fixed and never changing gallery of bequeathed art and artefacts, all of which need maintaining and kept clean. Something has to give.

I dare say his majesty would like us women on the committee to knuckle down to cleaning rather than giving him a hard time about the accounts and future plans to keep the place going. We are not flower arrangers at a church dear, we are all career women, who now choose to support this museum, using our areas of expertise.

We have to have a strategy, but he wouldn't know one if hit him in the proverbial……… He has fallen into this kind of work after a few years at Eton and then Cambridge. It's like this is his little baby, and he will not let it go. None of us want to take control from him even, we just want what is best for the place, and an equal say as committee members, but as always this has just become a battle of the sexes. I wonder sometimes whether he has engineered an almost all women committee to smooth his passage when it comes to managing the whole place himself.

Why not let' s see what happens if we all walk……… or should I say train.

31. Murder Is A Business. (m)

People are such gullible shits…… I despise them. They deserve all they get. A murderer doesn't have to be frenzied in his or her attack. It can be done professionally, with skill and without emotion. It's a business transaction. Don't get me wrong. I'm not for hire. Where would the fun be in that? No, I do it for me. Keep it simple that's what I think. No contract to worry about. No customer services. No consumer rights. Just me and my little murdering business. The Federation of Small Businesses doesn't have a job description that even remotely matches mine. I am off the tax radar too.

How can this be? I see you wondering. Well let me explain.

I do what is known in the trade as playing the system. It's easy. It avoids changes in circumstances because my first and so far, only victim is my new wife.

Perfect isn't in it!

I met her 8 months ago at a wedding. These events are perfect for effecting a business relationship. Of course, she had no idea I was in the murdering business………… and that she was going to be my first job.

Anyway, I digress.

I snared her over the copious glasses of champagne and after the DJ had created his best slow dance magic. It was really that easy. Women are suckers for all this shit. They believe the hype.

BOOM! she was hooked. As far as she knew the ultimate romantic meeting and the future was being mapped out and all society's rituals were driving her to her doom. We dated. We fought a little, a contrition that guarantees a massive trust winning bonus, we announced our engagement. We had a party like no other, money well spent, I think. Every event makes it less and less likely she will walk away; the stupid woman was trapped. Wedding plans ensued and then everyone else felt they owned us and our future, so it was simple from here on in.

The marriage went off without a hitch. I didn't pay for it of course, so no outgoings there. We settled down to domesticity after the whirlwind courtship. Now I was in the actual murder phase. I was all sweetness and light, attentive, smiley and courteous. I just had to figure out how to do it.

I find a mind map helps at such times. So I got some mind mapping software on the laptop and started planning. I didn't want anything long and drawn out. I'm an impatient bastard and anyway if she is gonna die she may as well sooner rather than later. These things can take months even years to set up and I only have so much time to get through the optimum amount of clients. You see I get to keep the house, the cars, the money in the joint account. All I have to do is make it look like an accident and that is easy to do, because wives are usually unsuspecting if you treat 'em well.

It would be telling to reveal how I did it but needless to say it's done. My first job was a great success. I could retire soon.

What was it I said at the beginning?

Oh yes........gullible shits.

32. My Cabaret. (m)

It's *Vilkommen* you twat. Not *Welcommen*.

Did you hear that? He can't even pronounce the words of the opening song. What a fuckin' tosser. What was the director thinking? Oh let me think, what was he thinking? I know, a bit of young ass… well, young-*ish*. That must be the value placed on this starring role. The director of course was around during Noah's flood by the look of him, so anyone under 65 is totally young meat. *(peering into the auditorium)* Hope he was worth it! That's to both of you wankers.

Nothing quite like short changing the audience for a piece of action. If you make yourself interesting, and spout a load of sycophantic bullshit, you get noticed. This crabby old director's ego has had a good old stroking by the look of it. *(pause)*

Look at his posture! *(incredulous)* He could be playing a bumbling yokel; his diction is diabolical. *(whispering)* You are supposed to be arching that back you idiot. Do you know nothing at all? Posing is the MC's role. He is the ultimate poseur. Everything needs to be exaggerated. *(posing as it should be done)* Oh come on please, you need a rod up your arse or something. Just remember what it was like as the director gave you one. Disgusting thought! Think about what your lower back and hips were doing. Tip that pelvis you fool. Or just maybe you don't have it in you.

Alright, I know I am not in the flush of youth but this fucker looks as though his arthritis is flaring up. He has a certain beauty I suppose, if you don't look too close, but he he's got no *charisma*. His performance is like a fuckin panto. The oaf could be playing Widow Twanky for all the relevance he is bringing to the part. You need irony and sarcasm you fool. It's not a working men's club! People have paid good money to actually watch something properly entertaining.

Why on earth I didn't get the part, I will never know. Always the understudy never the star. I have talent after all. I know how to research a role and give it depth. I would never resort to the 'directors couch' though - I thought my raw talent would have been enough. I've made a few mistakes in my career but it seems not shaggin' the director was the biggest by far.

Oh I can't watch. (*masking his eyes*) This saddens me so much. I feel sorry for the audience... oh and me of course. This role could have been my big breakthrough. West End! Broadway, here I come. I'm ready! "*Mein Damen und Herren ,Mesdames et Messieurs, Ladies and Gentlemen!*".... (*arms outstretched*)

(*sighs*)... Instead I'll probably end up being the third tart on the left, Helga - the one with the terrible wig and laddered stockings.

Look at what I've come to!

(*sings*) 'TwoLadies... twiddly diddly fucking dee...'

33. Nine Lives Of A munitions Worker. (f)

Your country needs you!

Just like our men folk, being herded off to the Front. We women suddenly had importance.
No sign of the vote yet of course but that is not surprising.

We have always been needed never much appreciated!

So now we are in the munitions factories, thousands of us, doing war work. It is war work too..........we could lose our health or die for our country, just like our men. Here are the threats to our wellbeing, the nine life threats:

TNT poisoning which could lead to death - yellow as a canary I got, and some of me mates died.

A variety of health hazards both environmental and physical - There was no Health and Safety back then.

Extremely Noisy conditions - You couldn't hear yourself think - I'm deaf now. would ya believe it.

Being blown up - Our factory blew up; it made the newspapers but many others didn't - all to do with morale they said.

Long hours - No social life I can tell ya, 12-hour shifts did for that.

Short or sometimes no breaks - We'd be gasping for food, a beer or a fag by the end of a shift, if we didn't get a break or two.

Repetitive yet dangerous work - I suppose this sounds a bit daft but after the war we women had a lot to put up with and often the work had already done for us mentally.

Strict rules which must be adhered to - A lot of us girls got in trouble at the beginning. No jewellery allowed, no shoes with any metal in 'em, we had to wear wooden clogs instead and no matches for our crafty fags.

And finally, as I said before

We have always been needed never much appreciated.

The worst thing for me and many of us munitions girls was the hostility of the men. Bleeding helping 'em out and all we got was *abuse!* Bloody cheek.

34. Of Course, I Am To Blame. (m)

"What happened?"

That's what almost everyone said apart from my oldest friends who all, to a man and woman, said

"What took you so fucking long?"

(looking sarcastically)

Both parties of course were operating from the fact that I left him. He was making sure that his friends thought only of what a bastard I was being.

What hurt most was all these friends dumped me, choosing to believe him and his narrative.

(sobbing gently)

In a way I did leave him... well when you look at it I did, or at least I was the one who had sufficient integrity to do so. But. When I tell you of the options, he gave me it may not seem so clear cut.

(settling himself down)

You see my man is gonna be a priest. "That's a stumbling block already" I hear you say.

Well that's just for starters.............

We had been together for years and of course when he said he wanted to train for the priesthood I said of course I would support him, isn't that what partners do?

(looking lovingly)

We spent much time talking the situation through and about the Church of England's stance on gay priests. I did this because I still believed that our relationship was worth fighting for and I wanted him to be sure about this institution he so wanted to join.

Things just got worse though. He knew that he would have to move to a parish as a curate once he was ordained but............of course I would not be able to move with him. He then insisted that I take a lodger so as to keep the house going and the mortgage paid up. I asked him did he expect me to give up my home life to a stranger and without a beat he said "YES, that was the only way to keep *our* house".

You see he'd thought it all through!
(angry now and then sad)

Finally, on the last of many weekends away to study, it being the last one before ordination, he showed me a letter from the bishop before he left, which basically said that he must renounce his relationship with me if he wished to be ordained.

(trying to catch his breath)

"There's nothing I can do about it", he said as he slammed the door and trounced off to catch his train.

(breaking down in tears)

I allowed myself this weekend to be in bits and then on Monday evening I............

35. Painted Lavvy. (f)

Oh I can't decide. Lavender Mist or Canyon Rose. Do you think that's from the Grand Canyon?
I always thought that those paint makers found these exotic colours in actual places, but they'd have to go a long way to get SunStar.

The upstairs bathroom has just been done, well a couple of years ago. I did it in Light Chartreuse in Flat. There's only the two of us now, so not much footfall.

But with the football,l that's different altogether. I'm looking for a colour for our downstairs privy. It must be twenty years since it was distempered. It wasn't due you understand. But. You see he's invited all the neighbours and blokes from the pub to come and watch the World Cup Final, and if I know that lot they'll be wanting the lavvie as much as you like. I've told him only small cans of beer, once they get pints down em there'll be hell to pay. I've told him no one, I mean no one is to use the upstairs bathroom.

(Pause)

Or maybe its Dresden Blue or Chelsea Blue. Do I go Flat again or Semi-lustre? I suppose semi-lustre will be easier to clean in case of accidents.

That's the problem with all these choices. I won't go anywhere near *Dulux*, their card has got 200 colours on it. I go all goggle-eyed when I see that in the shop. No its *Berger* for me.

It said on the card that the colours are intermixable so maybe if I buy a pint of each I can mix away. It could be fun and a bit exclusive. It still doesn't help me make a choice though.

(looking worried)

I wonder if we'll win the Cup? As we'll have a new *downstairs* you know. I'm not sure I want a win. They'll all stay here for a party if they do and my Light Chartreuse will be in real danger then. You know what drunk blokes can be like and I don't want to be bottom stair monitor all day and night.

You know it's best to be on the safe side. I've decided. I'm going to go for………………

FLAMINGO!

36. Rabbit Stew. (m/f)

The stew itself was a fatty and congealed mess, I wouldn't have served that stew with a fig compote. Fruity and fatty. Urgh! Good job there was plenty of wine flowing oh and the baguettes, I love so much were stacked high, "to dip in the juice" she suggested.

(grimacing)

Sculptures made from old books, were so close to my plate that I worried for their artistic integrity. Is gravy really a recognised arts medium I thought. A pile of china plates hovered at the edge of the small table too, as though waiting for the hordes to turn up or as an army of receptacles for the baguettes. Kitsch ornaments and religious icons were juxtaposed with wet laundry hanging everywhere.

She was also determined to speak only French in an effort to teach me. The fact I clearly did not understand much did not seem to faze her. On she went.

Still I had the stew!

Marie-Louise was in such a flap that I wondered why she had invited me. She flitted from subject to subject, rising from her chair endlessly to show me this or that and offering me more of the STEW .

Suddenly she stood up and exclaimed "A glass of whiskey, have a glass of whiskey. "

"Erm,………..Oh no I couldn't" I said. Grape and grain mixed, I don't think so. But then I thought perhaps the whiskey will break down the fat and it is good to accept what your host offers you.

(pause)

What in a sense connected us both, was us being artists, although I have to say very different ones. She had it seemed made this whole evening with that in mind. A kind of meeting of minds.

Oh well, it was kind thought. I had found a new friend after all and she seemed happy.

As I began to sip my whiskey, slowly so as to avoid many more mouthfuls of the stew I glanced over to a dark corner and was able to make out a pair of eyes. Large doleful eyes looking out from a hutch. Mrs. Rabbit was staring at me as I picked at her husband's bones…………

Oh, a perfect end to an *interesting* evening.

37. Regrets. (f)

Dead! *(Long Pause)* I am fucking dead. These weeds are for my girl. But they are also for me. There is nothing else left for me. How can I pick up the fucking pieces now? Death is now my garment of choice. I haven't seen her for 23 years, I'm here now though aren't I. That has to count for fucking something. More than he is. The bastard.

So many fucking men cannot face responsibility. He left us 25 years ago and has never bothered with her since then, or me for that matter. His solution to our problem was to leave us in the fucking lurch. I always thought the bastard would come back. I've waited all this time and still no sign. I'm a fool.

I wish I could understand how I got things so fucking wrong.

That's bloody men for you. You find a good 'un and they end up worse than the bad-uns. My dad was the same, so I shouldn't be surprised. He was a bastard to my mother. He deserted her eventually, didn't stop him pestering me though. The old cunt.

I am here alone; this is the sum of my daughter's life. No bastard father here. No fucking family here either, they all left when she was born disabled and wasn't what they expected. Never let it be said blood is thicker than water. I had to manage as best I could until it wore me out.

(pause)

I can fool myself that I did it for her, let her go I mean, but actually it was mostly to keep my sanity and some ounce of freedom for myself. It is hard to admit that but it is true.

Dear God! I did what you asked of me you fuckin old cunt ,ya!

(shaking her fist)

I got rid of her, but you never told me the guilt of that would wipe out the gesture. I was fooled by you, you old bastard.

Fuck em them men, that is what I always say now. I haven't always been like that, but the pain and the guilt sometimes has made me a bitch. The bastards can grind you down sometimes.

(suddenly turning to look beyond)

What the fuck! What the fuck are you doing here? How dare you? Thirty fucking years! ...

38. Saving A Life. (f)

Seven Hundred Jews! That's what it took to save a life. My life.

(barely regretful)

My brother. That bastard had never forgiven me for taking up with a woman and leaving my husband.

(looking proud)

He alienated me from our father, I had always been his favourite, the eldest child, the golden girl.

(suddenly sad)

I struggled to get my hat shop started up, but eventually I made it and was successful until the fucking Nazis arrived and took it from me. Oh not 'cos I was a lesbian, no it wasn't that. You see I am a Jewess and they didn't think a Jew should be in business in Amsterdam.

(looking incredulous)

I didn't hate them though. You see, I was convinced, wrongly as it turned out, that some of my Jewish clients had denounced me probably, or so I thought, to save their own skins.

(grimacing)

Funny isn't it?

A couple of years after I was closed down, I was grabbed on the street after a Resistance bombing. They knew I had known a couple of the people involved you see. I knew them of course but I didn't even know they were in the Resistance. Still these damn Nazis didn't believe me and I was facing the firing squad.

(looking fearful)

But. At the last minute they offered me a lifeline…… can you guess what it was?

I agreed to become a collaborator, betraying Jews, as many as I could. It was easy, me being a Jewess, I'd offer to find these people a safe house and when they arrived the Gestapo would be there waiting. I did this for quite some time and lived well off the Nazis as a result.

Towards the end of the Occupation though it became obvious to me that I needed to dig deeper to find where people might be in hiding, I was under immense pressure to clear out the remaining Jews, even me. I became desperate and was lucky enough to get some intelligence about a couple of families hiding in Prinsengracht. That's right! One of those I betrayed was Anne Frank. Quite a coup as it turned out, as last year her damn diary was published.

Now as I sit here awaiting my own execution. It is ironic that after all I did to survive the Nazis, my own country is the one to kill me. Yes, the only female collaborator to be executed and unlike the closure of the hat shop this *was* because I am a lesbian.

39. Speaking Out. (f)

I knew it had to be done. I had to move forward and strike a blow for female emancipation and I mean a bloody blow.

I worked in the damn mills, quietly fuming at the injustice of it all. But I'd reached a point of no return. No bloody more! I thought.

My Dad Horatio, a mill winder, was and still is, a supporter. Bless him.

This helps a lot! I know many lasses whose Dads or husbands are dead set against bloody *Votes for Women.*

This hanging onto the old ways and the beliefs of the upper classes makes me sick. They're nothing but jumped up bastards.

Bloody politicians after all and still they won't even speak with us. So, what do they expect us to do?

Working class lasses are beneath their contempt it seems and the *ladies* with us, don't do much better.

The day dawned in Manchester when that Grey chap was going to speak at a Liberal rally. These bloody people never expect anyone to speak when they are speaking. They think its a bloody cheek. But we activists were determined to get our point across. Christabel Pankhurst and me started to heckle him almost from the very start.

His face! You should have bloody seen it! He didn't like it........ and nor did the menfolk around us mostly. We carried on though and we got more and more excited and louder of course so the whole hall could hear us.

"Votes for Women" we chanted over and over until we were roughed up by the bobbies, taken away and arrested.

Bloody cheek, I thought.

The judge, the pompous old git, said "You can either give up the protesting or go to prison".

Prison it was then, best thing ever - it rallied women to our cause and started of the militant work of the Suffrage Movement as it became known.

You HAVE to speak out……..

40. Splitting The Difference. (m)

You know the type. "I'll do it, I know how to chop a tree down. It's all physics."

I should have known!

(slamming his head with his palm)

The tree was taller than the house and stood a mere 10 feet from it. The garden sloped towards the house too.

Derek told me that you had to cut the tree on the side facing away from the house so as to avoid it falling on the roof. I got this in theory but there were some other factors to take into consideration, but there was no getting through to him. Much as I tried to suggest things, Derek's temper was beginning to get the better of him, and believe me when he was like that you did not argue.

"If you think you can do any better…." he snapped.

His one act of appeasement though was to suggest we lash the tree trunk to another tree further down the garden. I was still not convinced but he, as I said before, knew best!

The tree was now lashed to large oak tree after a crash course from Derek on how to tie a particular knot. Aren't people bloody annoying sometimes? I was then waiting there as Derek started to attack with his chain saw. It did not take long however to see that we may have some potential trouble, so I bravely straddled the rope between the two trees to be able better to bring all my weight behind the tree being cut, if needed.

Derek continued to split the difference with the tree and suddenly, the beast lurched away from the cut and towards the house.

"Derek, look out" I shouted, taking the full weight of the tree, but he couldn't or wouldn't hear me. His wife stood up from where she had been sitting and shouted at him which broke his reverie and he then realised what was about to happen. He was like a rabbit in the headlights now, with no idea how to solve this particular problem.

The problem with all of this though, was the fact that I was straddling the rope between the trees still and this could mean I would *split my own difference* if something was not done and soon or even end up being catapulted into the neighbours garden.

I shouted at all the assembled spectators to rush off to other neighbours houses to ask for assistance, which seemed to take forever and in fact resulted in no one coming.
"Fuck" I shouted as both Derek, hanging onto the slain tree and I, now acutely aware of my own impending castration.

Thank heavens for old rope as suddenly the now cut tree swung towards the house it broke, thus relieving my gonads from being separated from each other and me.

41. The Artist (m/f)

He came into my life……………when was it now?

(looking curious)

I don't remember, it doesn't matter anyway. I was already an artist and had been for as long as I could remember.

(looking nonchalant)

But. He changed everything.

(excited)

He sat on my shoulder and told me what to do all the time, not in a shouty way, just gently and immediately. I took his instruction well and found I was more and more pleased with my art.

(looking proud)

There was a lack of urgency suddenly, everything ran in slow motion now and it felt great.

I knew my self better and realised I could stand still and simply do the work without effort or worry. It is enriching when you realise that you are bigger than the sum of your parts.

Much bigger.

I was for the first time a professional, not in a business way, but just in feeling sure of my skills.

All those terrible barriers to my success evaporated and I felt secure. Secure enough to jump to the next level, to the final opening of my- self to who I am.

The artist still travels with me and I appreciate and celebrate him and his effect on me. He has changed though from being on my shoulder to ……………….

being in my heart.

42. The Fairer Sex. (f)

All I wanted was to get way from Papa. Mama took acid after she found out about Papa's philandering. It was her only way out I suppose.

(cold manner)

Papa was a dairy man. Unglamorous work and beneath me, hence my excitement with the Hitler Youth. For the first time in my life I felt important. We female Nazis were afforded a special place in the heart of the Fuhrer.

(proud)

I tried to get work as a nurse, but the authorities would have none of it and after a few years of trying to escape, I found myself in exactly the same job as Papa. I was horrified. Was this all there was to be for me? This did not match my dreams, for a bright future as a daughter of the Fatherland and in following my destiny as a war worker war rather than motherhood.

(determined)

Those Jewish bastards had stolen all the work until we stopped them, and by the time I was 18, there was a need for us women of true strength. So I tried again to be a nurse and I was sent to Ravensbruck Concentration Camp instead. I didn't want to do this work but it was employment after all and in Germany that was everything.

After some time, I realised the work made me feel good about myself. I was paid well, had a uniform and the boots and whip particularly excited me. I was for the first time in my life in a position of control. Here I was working with *Kike* and other women, who were enemies of the State. I was just doing my work for the Fuhrer after all. I had to be strong, it was expected of every German woman, either as mother or worker.

It was I who had the power of life and death now, especially at Auschwitz. I was the boss in relation to women. I took part in the selection at the ramp and elsewhere, and took great pleasure in herding these women like cattle; I was used to that after all. I never had used a whip on cattle before though and was enraptured by this as I was by the random killing of inmates depending on my mood. Because all these people were sub-human, they deserved all they got and I was proud to operate this pest control for the Fatherland.

43. The Grass Is Greener. (m)

I'm a business man. I have to make sensible decisions with this in mind. What was good for business in 1878 was, in 1889 not remotely useful anymore. My father in law had left a tangled web of affairs at his death, with my wife as his executor and although I loved her, she had to be sent back to England. *(his head in his hands as he rests, dying, on a chaise)*

Firstly, she was like I am now - consumptive and having lost our only child last year and her father 18 months ago, needed rest and recuperation by the sea. Secondly, I was by then a renowned entrepreneur, feted at International Trade Fairs, friends with Vuitton and Hermes, with clients from the echelons of royalty and the aristocracy. I could no longer be seen with a wife who was ill and, let's be honest here, quite a liability, as someone with less social graces than one needs in the society I was to be found in. *(buries his head in the pillow)*

I took some advice from friends and associates in the Lodge and I then determined to send her to Bournemouth, where the church has a well-appointed rest home for those in the final stages of tuberculosis, She was to be fine there I was assured and I had no real need to visit her, as she was to be well taken care of.

What about you? You may ask. Without a helpmate in your life. How could your business prosper?

Well thanks to Mrs. Lewis, an actress friend, *(said with pride)* I now found that my business was growing as it should have been before. She was a woman of great style and perspicacity. She knew how businessmen operate, both professionally and personally. I must say how grateful I am to her, and I count all the expenses she accrued on my behalf, as money well spent. The jewels and clothing she needed to maintain a certain standard in society and the furniture that was needed in our apartment in *Rue Chaillot* was as nothing compared to the business benefits of having this beautiful, glamorous and lively woman on my arm.

Alas now, here in 1893 I lie, dying myself, from the consumption. Perhaps God is judging me. Mrs. Lewis is a help but I sense that she is distancing herself from me as I slip away. She has been a boon in my recent life but I fear alas her role will not be judged as a shrewd investment on my part, but I do hope that she can walk away from my death with some material comfort, *(fading in and out of consciousness)* She tells me she must leave soon as she has been booked into a prestigious New York theatre for the coming Summer season. She would often travel for her work even during our time together. I wish her well.

Poor poor Mary, my dear wife, left us in 1891 and it with some remorse that I make peace with God and confess to my weakness. I am a mere mortal after all and I did the best very best I could by her, but I should think she would rather have had me there with her than have me keep sending the fees for her care in that terrible parochial town.

Adieu my dear Mary. *(pause)* Au revoir sweet Alice. You were the two better sides of me.

44. The Interview. (f)

This job needs a particular type of person.

(smiley)

I suppose this interview has turned out differently to what you had in mind.

(pitying look)

It's good that your nodding, otherwise the taser will have to come out again and I am sensing that you don't want that.

(teacherly)

It's such a shame it took you so long to realise that resistance is futile. Your punters won't give in…………… what they want they get.

So you see you have to be ready because a 'safe word' doesn't figure with your clients.

That's why you get paid so well. Think of it as compensation. Death is not guaranteed after all, so you'll need money to carry on in life.

I can see that terror in your eyes and I would feel the same if I were in your shoes.

But as you can see, I am not.

(smug)

I've given you just a taste of what you can expect when you join our little exclusive club.

You will be joining, won't you?

Sorry I didn't quite get that?

(pause where she looks disappointed with the interviewee)

That's good I knew you'd see it my way, everyone does in the end.

Oh come on. No one in their right mind could expect to get £10k for a single session without making some small sacrifice.

Was it so bad? Its not like its real torture. Well ok the taser is a bit unpleasant but that wasn't even part of the session so you have to be ready for much worse than that.

Think though you'll be able to watch your punter's pleasure and you won't be able to disturb his fun with any kind of screams or pleas for help.

The gag is quite effective isn't it. It goes down well with everyone who uses our services.

Oh don't cry, they won't like that either. It's a bit premature anyway.

Shall we continue now…………………………………….

45. The Queue. (f)

A bakery. An Important place.

(looking proud)

Everyone needs bread. It's what I make.

(sure of herself)

You have to have a will of iron to make bread for customers day in day out. It's a commitment, even a vocation some would say.

(looking pious)

So when we were occupied by the damn Germans I shot off straight away to have my license stamped by the Nazi machine. They were only to happy to oblige as what I said before applies to them too.

We all need bread after all.

(confident)

Now I have always run a tight ship in the serving of my customers. The best thing I have found is the queue. No matter who you are in my view the queue takes precedence above all things. First come first served. Most people appreciate my system.

Now with the advent of the Occupation, a Dutch Nazi, an NSB, called Femcke thought she could try pushing in, claiming as a Dutch Nazi official she had the right to be served first. Well as you can imagine I was having none of it. I told her straight, to get back in line, because if the queue was disturbed then anarchy would ensue.

She started to threaten me with all sorts of punishment for this out-rage but I was refusing to back down even though the others in the queue were becoming agitated. Suddenly out of nowhere an SS man appeared. There was a hush. Both me and this damn woman I could see were up for the debate, neither of us willing to back down.

"What is going on here" The SS man said. I remained silent. It's the best way at times like this.

"I was just saying to this woman how important it was for us officials to be served promptly." the bitch asserted. She looked sure of her-self.

"No, no" shouted the SS man.

"The queue cannot be disturbed, we do not want to encourage anar-chy, now do we?"

A ripple of stifled giggles could be heard, thankfully not by the SS man, who stood in the doorway. This was a tense event as I was sure that many other Nazis would have sided with her. BUT!!

"Come, as you were" he suggested and that damn NSB bitch was put back in her place for good.

46. Trapped. (m)

(lying in bed on his back with just the light from a bedside clock)

My head is whizzing around. Well not my head as much as my thoughts inside it.

(turns over and faces the light source)

All of 'em going nowhere. One leads to the next. No one here to talk to. Isolated in the middle of the night.

No way to gain clarity about where I find myself.

(rubbing eyes)

Oh bugger I'm not supposed to do that.

If I could be bothered, I'd get up and wash my hands and eyes.

We humans are so instinctive. We cannot help ourselves. It's how we have passed this virus around after all.

Look no hands touching any part of me.

(jazz hands)

Yes, I'm in bed, obviously. It's 3am. I should be asleep, sorting all this dangerous shit out in my sub-conscious but not tonight. Seems being trapped is where we are all at. This is my daily blip in lockdown, I have one every day.

"You've got a bed" I hear you say, and that's true, I am fortunate. I know that.

It's just I am one bill away from disaster. Well maybe not really, but at 3am here in my bed it feels like it. Only the daytime really helps. That's a time to sort things out in my head with the sun on my back.

But. No sunshine today. Just rain reinforcing my mood of doom. I'm holding out for Sunday when the sun is shining, or so the weather forecast says. Let's hope that that forecast is more accurate than the latest COVID projections are. No one knows to be honest, we all know that.

It helps to speak it all out loud though. Funny how fear when its inside, can mount and mount and mount. Just five hours to go and then I can start to sort stuff out again.

(turns over to face other way)

47. The Joys Of A Tiara (f)

Persian? You mean Iranian? Who knew? My how things change, that is fashion for you.

T_I_A_R_A. Tiara is a Persian word. Persian kings used to wear them. Not so pretty as me I bet.

(turning her nose up and adjusting her tiara)

Isn't this interesting?

(setting herself up to make a pronouncement)

For me Tiara's are pure Disney, I mean Cinderella wore one, Snow white too and even her wicked stepmother had a kind of plain one.

(pause)

Anyway, her's was masculine in flavour so I don't think it counts, perhaps it was designed with a Persian king in mind.

(grimacing)

You know I look at crowns, and sometimes people mistake tiaras for crowns, and they're just not practical. I mean how could I possibly run around as I do, with a crown perched on my head. A crown simply has no grip. Whereas with a tiara you have hair to adhere to or the backs of one's ears. So much more useful when being something more than a seated princess.

There are too many tiaras in the world to describe here but one I think deserves a special mention, it appeals to my tomboy nature.........its one from the fourth century in China and it is especially important as it actually looks like a helicopter, with blades and branches, and encrusted with flowers made from precious stones. I look at it and I think wouldn't it be wonderful if those blades and branches spun around so any princess could fly.

(looking down)

The closest I'll get to such an adventure is wearing a tiara when I go hunting wild beasts in my own garden……………..HA!

48. The Devil Is On My Shoulder.(f)

Isn't it ok for me to feel down now and again? We all face issues in our lives sometimes don't we?

You know often, when someone tries to cheer me up, I get so pissed off. It's like offering chocolate to a diabetic when they are scared about going to the hospital. Just not what they need right now. If you're going to be a real friend, pack it in with the acme remedies.

And. Definitely do not give me something for what you think ails me and then run out of the room? That is the worst thing you can do. It makes me feel this small.

(pinching her fingers together to show just how small)

Just think please! Homemade remedies should be left where they can be found by a person in need. We all have Google don't we? The remedies can be gently referenced if you must, but please *please* do not come to me with your smiling countenance, and your pushing you chin up at me. You know that makes me want to play to the stereotype and kill you.

(acting thrusting a knife into someone)

You clearly don't understand what is going on for me. and much as I appreciate your attempts at counselling or personal development, please save the quackery for someone who gives a fuck. Go and start a QVC channel, become a guru or write a fucking book. Just get out of my face.

Don't get me started about the church's role in the lives of people with mental health issues. I used to be a church goer, quite an avid one to be honest, I wouldn't say it actually fed me, that wine and those crackers……Urgh! but there were other people like me there who sometimes outside of church I could connect with.

The final straw for me though was one day when our pastor with whom I had just had a long chat about how I was feeling, actually pointed to me during a service and said, wait for it………….

"The Devil is on that Woman's Shoulder; I think she needs to find somewhere else to explore her pain. "

"Amen" said the bleating congregation……..

(pause looking shocked, stunned and disbelieving)

"Amen…….." said I as I walked away.

49.Who's In Charge? (f)

Who's in charge? I am of course! Of course! I am.

I run this house. I make sure my kids are fed. The bog is clean. Oh yeah, both of them. I deal with the bills, sort the school out when stuff goes wrong there and believe me that is more often than I would like. I am in charge of our lives. Honest!

Yet why do I so often feel out of control. I sit here with his nibs every night watching what he wants to watch on the box. He often looks over and smiles, like that's enough in this fucking boring existence to keep me happy.

It's 9 o'clock. He smiles again and nods in the direction of the kitchen, like I have nothing better to do, cups of tea, four sugars and cheese on toast. He seems to live for that moment. I can tell you I don't. He often catches me daydreaming of a better and different life, one without him preferably.

"Come on girl!" he says with more enthusiasm than he ever shows about anything else. "It's time."

A few weeks back I tried to talk to him about how I feel. I made a mistake in thinking he would lift his head up from *The Chase,* to listen to his wife, his significant other, tell him about an Open University course she had found that she'd like to pursue. Seeing as I do such a good job at home, I thought a Business Administration course would suit me. I talked for a good five minutes and he motioned a couple of times to just wait a minute as 'The Chase' was on, and this time they were playing for £45,000.

What I couldn't do with that money I can tell you. You hear of couples breaking up when they win big, well I'd be one of those people, off like a shot. No more fucking cheese on toast.

It was only at the end that I realised he was watching a fucking repeat and that it was 9pm again. He'd seen this episode before and still he couldn't lift his head up. Off we go to the kitchen once more. I stood there, motionless, not understanding what I had come to. Automatic pilot kicked in then and before I knew it, I was sitting down watching him gorge himself on his nightly treat. Yet something had snapped in me when the toast had popped out of the toaster.

As I settled back down it dawned on me that the only way to get him to listen was do what I do best and take charge.

So here I am single, successful and finally happy. I still do all the stuff I ever did before, but minus the cheese on toast.

Who's in charge?

Me, that's who.

50. Was Only Tryin' To Help...(m)

All I ever wanted was to help. This came about because I was being wonderfully creative and supportive in an integrated dance company. Sure, I ended up getting paid to work with this man which made a difference especially in the end. His Mum knew me, all about me in fact, even the gay bit. Her son had an inoperable brain tumour, so for years his Mum and Dad, with whom he lived, had been on a knife edge. They never knew when he might die. The doctors some 30 years before, had said this could happen at any time.

All boded well at the start. I guess they thought I would just take him places and give them some respite. They never in their wildest dreams thought I would start to teach him some rudimentary skills.

This went on for two years and with the parents' support, we were even moving towards him going away to a residential place for the blind - oh did I forget to tell you, he was blind?

The blindness was actually the only major issue for him, although his parents had him in a day centre for people with learning difficulties. As with so many people he was misdiagnosed and it had for years suited the family to have him dependent.

The more I worked with him the more it became clear to everyone, yes, even his parents, that they had let his diagnosis get in the way of progress. It's a funny thing, guilt and people's responses to it are even more so.

When it came to it, the Mum in particular suddenly dug her heels in over him going away. She began to say my agenda was to rip her son from the family, that he wasn't ready, he would never cope. I argued and argued, I felt bad on his behalf and also that his parents had wasted my time, just jollying me along, never intending to let their son go, even though he wanted to. Boy did he want to! Of course, the social worker who had set all this work up, just crumpled under the family's pressure.

"We must always see the families are on board" he said.

"What about the man's independence?" I said. "This was what this project was all about. Mum always said "the sky's the limit" for my son." What utter bollocks.

Then the bombshell was dropped. I didn't see it coming but should have known. It happens all too often. It seemed after all I had done for the family, the one thing they really couldn't stomach when the chips were down, was ....

.... me taking their son out for a dinner. With my husband.

Made in the USA
Middletown, DE
19 May 2020

95063345R00060